Compass Point

Phonics Readers

What Plants and Animals Need

by Nancy Leber

Reading Consultant: Wiley Blevins, M.A.
Phonics/Early Reading Specialist

 COMPASS POINT BOOKS
Minneapolis, Minnesota

Compass Point Books
3109 West 50th Street, #115
Minneapolis, MN 55410

Visit Compass Point Books on the Internet at *www.compasspointbooks.com*
or e-mail your request to *custserv@compasspointbooks.com*

Photographs ©: Cover and p. 1: Corbis, p. 6: Brand X Pictures/Nicole Katano,
p. 7: PhotoDisc/Doug Menuez, p. 8: Corbis/Lucidio Studio, Inc., p. 9: Capstone Press/Gary
Sundermeyer, p. 10: Bruce Coleman, Inc./Karen and Ian Stewart, p. 11 top: Unicorn
Stock/Russell R. Grundke, p. 11 bottom: Minden Pictures/Frans Lanting, p. 12: DigitalVision

Editorial Development: Alice Dickstein, Alice Boynton
Photo Researcher: Wanda Winch
Design/Page Production: Silver Editions, Inc.

Library of Congress Cataloging-in-Publication Data
Leber, Nancy.
    What plants and animals need / by Nancy Leber.
        p. cm. — (Compass Point phonics readers)
    Includes bibliographical references and index.
    Summary: Describes what plants and animals need to live, such as air and
    water, in a text that incorporates phonics instruction.
        ISBN 0-7565-0529-1 (hardcover : alk. paper)
        1. Life (Biology)—Juvenile literature. 2. Plants—Juvenile
    literature. 3. Animals—Juvenile literature. 4. Reading—Phonetic
    method—Juvenile literature. [1. Life (Biology) 2. Plants. 3. Animals.
    4. Biology. 5. Reading—Phonetic method.] I. Title. II. Series.
    QH325.L39 2003
        570—dc21   2003006374

Table of Contents

Dear Parent or Caregiver,

Welcome to Compass Point Phonics Readers, books of information for young children. Each book concentrates on specific phonic sounds and words commonly found in beginning reading materials. Featuring eye-catching photographs, every book explores a single science or social studies concept that is sure to grab a child's interest.

So snuggle up with your child, and let's begin. Start by reading aloud the Mother Goose nursery rhyme on the next page. As you read, stress the words in dark type. These are the words that contain the phonic sounds featured in this book. After several readings, pause before the rhyming words, and let your child chime in.

Now let's read *What Plants and Animals Need*. If your child is a beginning reader, have him or her first read it silently. Then ask your child to read it aloud. For children who are not yet reading, read the book aloud as you run your finger under the words. Ask your child to imitate, or "echo," what he or she has just heard.

Discussing the book's content with your child:
Explain to your child that animals have special body parts that take in air. Some animals, such as people and horses, have a nose and lungs. Other animals, such as fish, have gills that take in air from the water.

At the back of the book is a fun Word Bingo game. Your child will take pride in demonstrating his or her mastery of the phonic sounds and the high-frequency words.

Enjoy Compass Point Phonics Readers and watch your child read and learn!

4

A Diller, A Dollar

A diller, a **dollar,**
A ten o'clock **scholar,**
What makes you come so soon?
You used to come at ten o'clock,
And now you come at noon.

You may have pets at home
and in class. You may grow plants
in the yard, the garden, or in a
window box. What do plants and
animals need to live and grow?

A plant needs sunlight to live and grow larger. Most plants cannot live in a dark place. A plant gets light from the sun.

A plant needs soil and water.
Most plants get water from the soil.
The water in the soil comes from
rain and snow. The snow turns to
water as it melts.

A plant needs air to grow. Plants need 4 things. Plants need light, soil, water, and air.

The plant in the jar can grow. It has the 4 things a plant needs.

Like plants, animals need air to live and grow larger. Like plants, animals need water. Animals drink water. They clean up in it, too.

Animals need food. Some wild animals eat plants. Deer and rabbits eat grass and leaves.

Some wild animals eat meat. Tigers and lions hunt for meat.

Animals need a safe home.
A bird can make a home in a nest.
A fox can make a home in a den.
Animals need air, water, food, and a safe home.

Word List

r-Controlled Vowel (ar)

dark
garden
jar
larger
yard

Science

air
animals
food
soil
water

Word Bingo

You will need:
- 1 sheet of paper
- 18 game pieces, such as pennies, beans, or checkers

Player 1

dark	march	garden
larger	have	yard
farm	jar	are

14

How to Play

- Fold and cut a sheet of paper into 12 pieces. Write each game word on one of the pieces. The words are *are, dark, farm, garden, have, jar, larger, little, march, smart, star, yard.*
- Fold each piece of paper and put it in a bag or box.
- The players take turns picking a folded paper and reading the word aloud. Each player then covers the word if it appears on his or her game card. The first player to cover 3 words either down, across, or on the diagonal wins. You can also play until the whole card is covered.

Player 2

jar	star	larger
little	yard	garden
are	dark	smart

Read More

Dahl, Michael. *Do Cows Eat Cake? A Book About What Animals Eat.* Minneapolis, Minn.: Picture Window Books, 2003.

Frost, Helen. *We Need Water.* Mankato, Minn.: Pebble Books, 2000.

Royston, Angela. *Living and Nonliving.* My World of Science Series. Chicago, Ill.: Heinemann Library, 2003.

Stewart, Melissa. *Plants.* Simply Science Series. Minneapolis, Minn.: Compass Point Books, 2003.

Index